Table of Contents

MW01504162

The equation for Bayes Theorem is

$$P(A|B) = \frac{P(A) * P(B|A)}{P(B)}$$

Where

- A & B are events
- P(A) and P(B) are the probabilities of A and B without regard for eachother
- P(A|B) is the conditional probability, the probability of A given that B is true
- P(B|A) is the probability of B given that A is true

The equation is somewhat complicated, but using the equation really isn't. What it ends up being is just a normalized weighted average, given an assumption.   One of the goals of this book is to develop your intuition for these problems, so we will be discussing many of the problems from the normalized weight average perspective.

$$P(A|B) = \frac{\overbrace{P(A)}^{\text{Weighted Average}} * \overbrace{P(B|A)}^{\text{Assumption}}}{\underbrace{P(B)}_{\text{Normalized}}}$$

To solve all of these problems we will follow these steps

1. Determine what we want the probability of, and what we are observing
2. Estimate initial probabilities for all of the possible answers
3. For each of the initial possible answers, assume that it is true and calculate the probability of getting our observation with that possibility being true
4. Multiply the initial probabilities (Step 2) by the probabilities based on the new observation (Step 3) for each of the initial possible answers
5. Normalize the results (divide each probability by the sum of the total probabilities so that the new total probability is 1)
6. Repeat Steps 2-5 over and over for each new observation

Let's visualize this using a simple dice problem and using the area of rectangles to show relative probabilities

Example 1 – A Simple Example With Dice

Suppose that your friend has 3 dice. One has 4 sides, one has 6 sides, and one has 8 sides. He draws one die at random, rolls it one time without showing you, and reports the result as having rolled a 2. How would you calculate the probability that the die was the 4 sided die, the probability that it was the 6 sided die, and the probability that it was the 8 sided die?

One useful way to visualize this is as an area. The total area of this square is 1.0, which represents the 100% probability that we selected some die, and rolled it. Each column represents one of the possible dice selected. Each column has an area of .333 since each die has a 33.3% chance of being selected.

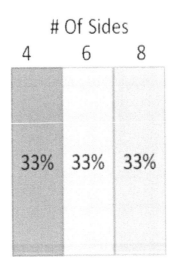

So far we haven't done Bayes Theorem. This is just a chart that shows the odds of selecting any given die from the bag.

After we select a die, we roll it and get some result. We can use our area chart to understand this step as well. We partition each column based on the possible outcomes. So the column associated with the 4 sided die gets broken into 4 equally sized rows. The column associated with the 6 sided die gets broken into 6 rows, and 8 rows for the 8 sided die.

Of Sides

4	6	8
1	1	1
	2	2
2	3	3
		4
3	4	5
	5	6
4		7
	6	8

Result of Roll

Interestingly, we still haven't used Bayes Theorem. This is the same chart we would make if I asked "Make a chart showing the odds of drawing each of the dice from the bag, and rolling all of the possible numbers." The part where we use Bayes Theorem comes when we input new results and use those results to update our probabilities.

In this case, the result is that we rolled a 2 with the selected die. With our chart, the way we use this information is to discard any outcome which doesn't match our result. I.e. discard all rolls that were not a 2. That looks like this

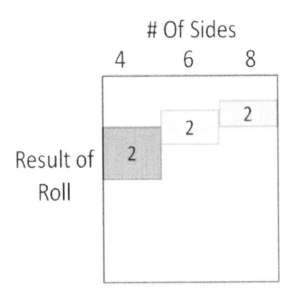

The only remaining results are times where we rolled a 2.

Our objective with Bayes Theorem is to now calculate the odds of each of our initial states, i.e. what die did we use. We can do that by normalizing our chart so that the total area filled is 1.0 again. Initially, the outcomes filled the full area. But right now we only see the portion of the outcomes associated with rolling a 2. We now want to update the chart to reflect the certainty that we did get that roll (because it was in the past)

So we divide the area of each cell by the total area of all 3 cells. This will ensure that the total area covered is 1.0.

We know the areas of each of the cells. The area of each column was initially 1/3. Within each column the area of the cells associated with the 4 sided die were 1/4 of that column, likewise the cells associated with the 6 and 8 sided die were 1/6 and 1/8 of their respective columns. So the area of the remaining cells are

- In the 4 sided die column: $1/3 * 1/4 = 1/12$
- In the 6 sided die column: $1/3 * 1/6 = 1/18$
- In the 8 sided die column: $1/3 * 1/8 = 1/24$

Summing those values results in a total area of 13/72. (as a side note, this means we had a 13/72 chance of rolling a 2 with a die drawn from this bag)

So our current total area is 13/72, and we need to scale that to get a final area of 1.0. We can get that by normalizing our results. That is, dividing each individual result by the total to make the total sum 1.0. Dividing by 13/72 is the same as multiplying by 72/13. So when we multiply the height of each cell by 72/13 what we get is

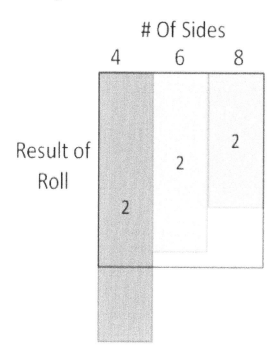

Just to make the graphing work, we can adjust the width of each column so that the area of each of the cells is unchanged, but that the height of all 3 columns is uniform. When we do that what we get is

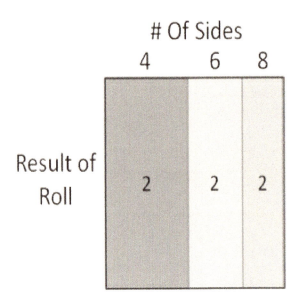

And here each column's relative area reflects its probability that it was the die chosen. In this case, the 4 sided die has 6/13 of the total area, the 6 sided die has 4/13 of the total area, and the 8 sided die has 3/13 of the total area. That's the final answer.

Here is a review of what we did before we show how to do the same problem as a table.

1) Determine the possible starting states. I.e. we could have selected a 4, 6, or 8 sided die

2) Estimate initial probabilities for each starting state. Here we assumed each state had an equal probability or a 1/3 chance

3) List all possible outcomes for each of the starting states

4) Multiply each outcome by the initial probability to get a probability of having that initial state **AND** that outcome

At this point, we haven't actually used Bayes Theorem, but we will on the next step

5) Discard all outcomes that don't match the new piece of observed information

6) Normalized (i.e. scale) the remaining probabilities so they add up to 1.0

The only simplification we will sometimes make to this process is instead of listing all possible outcomes (step 3 above) and then discarding the ones that don't match our observed new piece of information (step 4), we can just list only the outcomes that match our observed information (i.e. combine steps 3 and 4).

Let's do the same problem again as a table

Example 1 – Again, This Time As A Table

Step 1 – Determine Initial Possibilities

What we want is the probability of three different possibilities. Did we select a 4 sided, 6 sided, or 8 sided die?

Step 1
Die
4
6
8

Step 2 – Estimate initial probabilities

Once again, we will assume a uniform probability distribution, i.e. each die had a 1/3 chance of being drawn. A uniform probability distribution isn't always the best, but in this case, since we know we have three dice, making each of the three dice equally weighted is the obvious choice. This becomes column 2

Step 1	Step 2
Die	Initial Probabilities
4	1/3
6	1/3
8	1/3

Step 3 – For each initial possibility, calculate the chance of getting our observation

Our observation was that a 2 was rolled. If we assume that our friend had the 4 sided die, the odds that die would roll a 2 is 1/4. If we assume that our friend had the 6 sided die, the odds that die would roll a 2 is 1/6. If we assume that our friend had the 8 sided die, the odds that die would roll a 2 is 1/8

This is combining two previous steps "For each possibility list out all possible outcomes" and "Discard all outcomes that didn't match the observed new data"

Instead, what we are doing is, for each possibility individually, assuming it had been selected and then determining what the odds of getting the observed outcome are. In our area chart, this would have been the same as asking "What percentage of the column that it is in does this specific cell take up?"

For the 4 sided die, this is 1/4. I.e. if we had selected the 4 sided die, we would have a 1/4 chance of rolling a 2. The odds are 1/6 and 1/8 for the 6 and 8 sided die respectively. This goes into the third column

Step 1	Step 2	Step 3
Die	Initial Probabilities	Chance of Roll
4	1/3	1/4
6	1/3	1/6
8	1/3	1/8

Step 4 – Get the weighted average. Multiply initial probabilities by each probability based on the assumption.

This step is multiplying columns 2 and 3. In our graphic example, this would have been calculating the area for each of the remaining cells. The result for each cell here is equivalent to saying "What are the odds of drawing a 4 (or 6 or 8) sided die and rolling a 2 with it?"

Step 1	Step 2	Step 3	Step 4
Die	Initial Probabilities	Chance of Roll	New Probability
4	1/3	1/4	1/12
6	1/3	1/6	1/18
8	1/3	1/8	1/24

Step 5 – Normalize the Results

In this step, we need to scale our resulting probabilities so that they sum to 1.0. The total probability of picking one of the 3 dice, and rolling a 2 is $1/12 + 1/18 + 1/24 = 13/72$. So we know that the odds that we selected any of the dice and rolled a 2 are $13/72$.

This takes into account the fact that before rolling the dice, the odds of getting a 2 were below 100%, but now that we have that result, we need to adjust our odds to account for the fact that it already happened.

Normalizing each of the dice, we find the probability of each die being the one we selected to be:

- 4 sided die $= (1/12) / (13/72) = (1 * 72) / (12 * 13) = 6/13$
- 6 sided die $= (1/18) / (13/72) = (1 * 72) / (18 * 13) = 4/13$
- 8 sided die $= (1/24) / (13/72) = (1 * 72) / (24 * 13) = 3/13$

And that's the answer.

When we started the problem, we assumed that each die had a 33.3% chance that it was the one selected from the bag. After rolling a single time and observing a 2, we determined that the odds the 4 sided die was the one selected was 46.1%, the odds the 6 sided die was the one selected was 30.8%, and the odds the 8 sided die was the one selected was 23.1%.

If we had more die rolls, we could incorporate those results as well, using the new percentages as our starting percentages and really refine the numbers

This is the final resulting table. The odds that each die was the one selected are in the column on the far right.

Step 1 Die	Step 2 Initial Probabilities	Step 3 Chance of Roll	Step 4 New Probability	Step 5 Normalized Final Result
4	1/3	1/4	1/12	6/13
6	1/3	1/6	1/18	4/13
8	1/3	1/8	1/24	3/13
		Total Probability	13/72	

Some things to take note of for this example

There are a few points that we didn't hit in this example but are important to know

- When we calculated the chance of getting a roll for each die, the odds were 1 divided by the number on the die. But that is true only because we rolled a 2, which is a number that could be rolled by any of the dice. The true odds for each roll are 1 divided by the number on the die **IF** the number rolled is less than or equal to the number on the die. Otherwise, the odds for that die are zero. For instance, if we had rolled a 7, then we would show the odds of getting that result with the 4 sided die was zero, the odds with the 6 sided die was zero, and the odds with the 8 sided die was 1 / 8. When we normalized there would have been a 100% chance that the die that rolled the 7 was the 8 sided die
- For this problem, we worked with fractions, because they are fairly clean for only 3 possible dice, and only 1 roll. For most problems, with more possibilities and more data, fractions become a pain and it is easier to work with decimals.
- It is usually just as easy to find the probability for all possibilities as for a single possibility. i.e. If you want to find the probability of the 4 sided die for this problem, you might as well solve for the 6 and 8 sided dice at the same time since you have to do that anyway to get the total probability

What is in the rest of the book

At this point, you may feel that you have a good grasp of Bayes' theorem and wonder if it is worth reading the rest of the book. And it's a good question because overall Bayes' theorem is very simple, so if you want to put the book down and kick back with some coffee I can't blame you. For the most part, everything that is more complicated than what we just covered falls into only a few different buckets, either

- Making the initial probabilities more complicated to cover cases where you have detailed initial information or
- Making the conditional probabilities more complicated to cover real-life scenarios that are more complicated than rolling a dice or flipping a coin. (Like say, estimating the number of goals scored in a soccer game)

For the most part, this book is going to avoid doing either of those and focus on easier to understand, intuitive examples.   None-the-less there are some interesting intricacies that we'll cover that may not be obvious from the first example such as

- How to include more than one piece of data
- How to handle possible errors in the data
- Non-intuitive final probabilities in the real-life example of drug testing

Bayes Theorem Terminology

Up until now, we've skipped over some of the technical terminologies for Bayes theorem. Now it is time to go over it, if for no other reason than so that you will understand it when looking at other sources.

- The initial probability, the probability of each possibility before we see the new data, is called the **Prior**
- The normalized answer after computing the probability after incorporating the new data is called the **Posterior**
- The total probability that is used to normalize the answer is the **Normalizing Constant**
- The conditional probability, i.e. the probability of each possibility given the new data, is called the **Likelihood**

Looking at it in equation form

$$\underset{\text{Posterior}}{P(A|B)} = \frac{\overset{\text{Prior} \quad \text{Likelihood}}{P(A)*P(B|A)}}{\underset{\text{Normalizing Constant}}{P(B)}}$$

How that looks on the table for the first problem is

	Prior	Likelihood		Posterior
Step 1	Step 2	Step 3	Step 4	Step 5
Die	Initial Probabilities	Chance of Roll	New Probability	Normalized Final Result
4	1/3	1/4	1/12	6/13
6	1/3	1/6	1/18	4/13
8	1/3	1/8	1/24	3/13
		Total Probability	13/72	
		Normalizing Constant		

Example 2 – Testing For Illness

This example will show a different way to think about Bayes theorem to help you understand how it works. Bayes theorem can be visualized using a decision tree.

You are testing for an illness at a school. That illness might be chickenpox. You know that 20% of the students have that illness, and 80% of them are not sick. You do not know which specific students have chickenpox, which is why are you doing the test. You have a test for chickenpox that is right some of the time but also gives wrong answers some of the time. (Note, every single medical test does this with different rates of right answers vs. wrong answers). The correct answer vs error rate for the test is

- If they have chickenpox, the test will correctly report that they have it 70% of the time (True Positive)
- If they have chickenpox, the test will incorrectly report that they don't have it 30% of the time (False Negative)
- If they don't have chickenpox, the test will correctly report that they don't have it 75% of the time (True Negative)
- If they don't have chickenpox, the test will incorrectly report that they have it 25% of the time (False Positive)

Given this scenario, the question is: if you test a student, and the test comes back positive, what are the odds that they actually have chickenpox?

Initial Probability

Like all of the Bayes problems, we will start with initial probabilities. In this case, there are two possible initial states. Either the student has chickenpox or they do not. The initial probability that they have chickenpox is the probability of the entire school, which is 20%. There is an 80% chance that they don't have chickenpox.

Likelihood Function

Before we do any test, i.e. before using Bayes Theorem, We know there are 4 possible results after the test. We can show those results with a probability table. Those results are the product of the initial probability and the likelihood that the test will report a positive or a negative

- True Positive = 20% of students with chickenpox * 70% true positive rate = 0.14
- False Positive = 80% of students without chickenpox * 25% false positive rate = 0.2
- True Negative = 80% of students without chickenpox * 75% true negative rate = 0.6
- False Negative = 20% of students with chickenpox * 25% false negative rate = 0.06

As a table, that is

		Odds	
		Has Chickenpox	No Chickenpox
Test Is	Positive	0.14	0.2
	Negative	0.06	0.6

Since all those probabilities sum to 100%, we can also show this as a pie chart

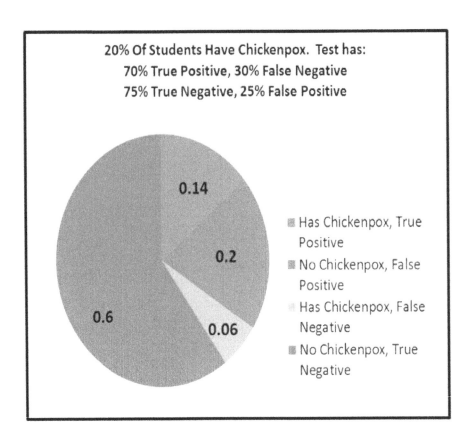

20% Of Students Have Chickenpox. Test has:
70% True Positive, 30% False Negative
75% True Negative, 25% False Positive

0.14

0.2

0.6

0.06

- Has Chickenpox, True Positive
- No Chickenpox, False Positive
- Has Chickenpox, False Negative
- No Chickenpox, True Negative

Incorporating The New Results

One way of thinking of Bayes theorem is that we are keeping a specific row of the probability table based on our new results. A different way to think of it is that we are choosing a path in a decision tree based on our results.

For instance, if we start with the initial probability pie chart and do a test, we can get one of two possible results. We can either get a positive or negative test result. That leads us to this decision tree.

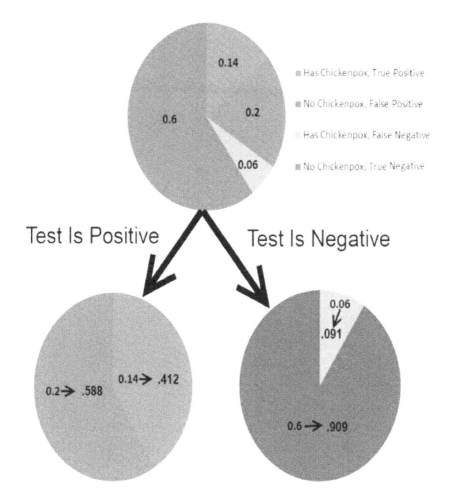

If the test is positive, we now only look at the outcomes where the test was positive. If the test is negative, we only look at the outcomes where our test was negative. This is like we split the 4 initial possible results into pairs of results, and then do the test to see which of the pairs we get.

In this case, the problem stated that the test came back positive. This means we go down the left path on the tree above, and are left with this result.

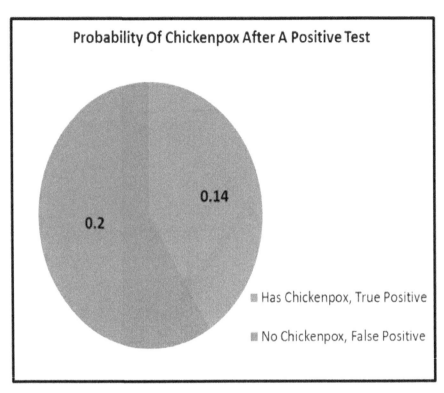

Probability Of Chickenpox After A Positive Test

- Has Chickenpox, True Positive
- No Chickenpox, False Positive

0.14

0.2

The two remaining results are that we either got a true positive or a false positive. When we made the initial probability table, the odds of either of those outcomes were 14% and 20% respectively. This has a total sum of 34%, which means that we expect to get a positive result 34% of the time.

After we do the test, however, we need to scale those probabilities up to equal 100%. This is because we now have the result, so there is a 100% probability that we did get a positive result. We can scale them up by dividing 0.14 and 0.2 by the sum of 0.34 and get this result.

		Odds		Sum
		Has Chickenpox	No Chickenpox	
Test Is Positive		0.14	0.2	0.34
Normalized		0.412	0.588	

As we see in the table, after getting a single positive test result, the odds that the student has chickenpox is 41.2%, with a 58.8% chance that they don't have chickenpox. So getting a positive result made it more likely that the student has chickenpox, with the odds going from 20% to 41.2%. But since the false positive rates and false negative rates are relatively high for this test (25% and 30%), getting a single positive test back didn't make it overwhelmingly likely that the student actually has chickenpox.

Disease / Drug / DNA Testing In Real Life

The chickenpox example was a made up problem. But it is applicable to many types of tests in real life. A person might get tested for a rare disease, one where the overall population has a 1% rate of having it. In that case, even if the true positive and true negative rates are relatively high, say (98% and 97%) the odds of having the disease after a single positive test are still only ~25%.

Many people are surprised to see that a positive result on the 98% reliable test still only means there is a 25% chance the person has the disease. Why was that surprising? **Because most people do not bake the initial probabilities into their intuition**.

We do a good job of understanding the conditional probability. After all, a 98% reliable test should make it much more likely the patient has the disease, which it does. **But if the initial probability is a really small number, the new probability will likely be small as well**. This often gets overlooked, and people implicitly assume an evenly distributed initial probability when thinking about these types of problems.

Overlooking the initial probability is the real joke behind this XKCD comic https://xkcd.com/1132/ (not having to pay the bet if the sun actually exploded is merely a bonus)

The best way to think of this is to remember that the final probabilities are the product of two numbers, the prior and the likelihood. If the prior is really small, chances are that the final result will still be fairly small after multiplying it by a single likelihood. If you get multiple results back, i.e. get positive results on several independent tests, and all of a sudden you are multiplying a single small prior by several large likelihoods, then a person will get the expected result that they likely have the illness.

This is applicable to things such as DNA testing as well. If a person has an extremely low initial likelihood of being the perpetrator of a crime, i.e. they are one person in a city of five million people and have no other indicators that would make them guilty, then a single positive DNA test has a strong likelihood of being a false positive.

The risk of false positives or false negatives is why you might get multiple tests done or multiple opinions from a doctor. Rolling in multiple new pieces of information can help make one possibility the overwhelmingly most likely outcome. The next example will show how to incorporate multiple new observations.

Example 3 – More Dice, More Rolls

Up until now, this book has shown examples of using Bayes Theorem to incorporate a single new piece of information, either the result of a die roll or a medical test. However, you can incorporate as many new pieces of information as you want, and typically the more information the better. (Frequently, additional data can overwhelm any errors you might have in estimating the prior probabilities or the likelihood probabilities)

This example goes back to dice and demonstrates how to incorporate multiple new pieces of information. However, that turns out to be simple. Essentially all we will be doing is repeating the same single step Bayes process that we just saw multiple times and using the output from one result as the input for the next result.

For this problem, we go back to trying to predict the probabilities of dice drawn at random. This time we are going have 6 possible dice, one with 4 sides, one with 6 sides, one with 8 sides, one with 10 sides, one with 12 sides and one with 20 sides. We are going to roll the die 15 times and calculate the probability that each die was the one that was drawn.

For this problem, since there is a lot more data, we will set up the problem in Excel to generate the probability tables. The tables that we will generate are like the table shown in the previous die problem, except transposed so that the possible dice run across the top row, and each new die roll is a new row. This makes for a nice format in Excel for multiple rolls and makes it easy to just set up the equations in one row and drag them down for the rest of the rolls.

Get the Excel File

If you want the Excel file shown, for this or any of the examples, it is available here for free. http://www.fairlynerdy.com/bayes-theorem-examples-v2

Generating The Random Roll

For the first dice problem, I chose that the die rolled a 2 as an illustrative example. However people are, in general, bad at picking truly random numbers, so instead of picking 15 "Random" die rolls, I input the 8 sided die as the one selected from the bag and let Excel choose random numbers to simulate the rolls using the function RandBetween().

The resulting 15 rolls were

6, 3, 2, 6, 8, 5, 6, 7, 2, 7, 7, 1, 5, 7, 6

Initial Probabilities

The first step is to decide the initial probabilities. Since there are six dice, and we are assuming they are randomly drawn from a bag, I set the initial probability of drawing each die to be 1/6, which is .1667

Dice Possibilities	4	6	8	10	12	20
Initial Probability	0.16667	0.16667	0.16667	0.16667	0.16667	0.16667

Likelihood Of Getting Each Roll

The next step is to set up the equation to determine the probability of getting any given roll for any given die. This equation needs to account for two possibilities

- If the die roll is greater than whichever die we are looking at, the probability that specific die would roll that number is 0. (i.e. if we rolled an 9, the probability that a 4, 6, or 8 sided die would roll that number is zero)
- If the die roll is less than whichever die we are looking at, the probability that specific die would roll that number is 1 divided by the number of sides on the die. (I.e. the probability that a 6 sided would roll a 3 is 1 in 6

Multiplying Initial Probabilities By Likelihood

The next step is to multiply the initial probability from the previous step by the likelihood of getting the observed roll. This is equivalent to getting an area for each remaining cell like we saw in the first example. Since we have multiple observations, the initial probability that we use is the final normalized probability coming out of each step. We only use the starting probability of 1/6 for each die for the first roll, after that we use the final normalized probability from the previous step.

If you were doing this manually you could account for the new observations and just pick which equation to use. Since we are doing this problem in Excel, we will use the If() function, which will let us use one likelihood equation or the other based on the observed roll.

Our final resulting equation in pseudocode for Excel is

= IF (roll > die # , 0, 1 / die number) * previous normalized probability

This equation says, if the roll is greater than the die number, set the probability equal to zero, otherwise set the probability equal to 1 divided by the die number. Then multiply that result by the previous normalized probability.

Normalize The Results

The final step is to normalize the results after each roll, which will give the total probability up until that roll

We can get the normalized result by summing all of our probabilities and then dividing each individual probability by that sum.

Final Result

What we end up with is that after the 15th roll, we calculate a 96.4% chance that we had selected the 8 sided dice and a 3.4% chance we had the 10 sided dice.   The 12 and 20 sided dice had a very small percentage, and the 4 and 6 sided dice had a zero percent chance.

This answer, of course, matches the fact that we input the 8 sided die into Excel's random number generator.

When we plot the percentages after each roll

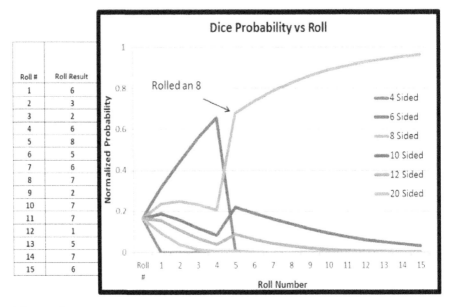

Roll #	Roll Result
1	6
2	3
3	2
4	6
5	8
6	5
7	6
8	7
9	2
10	7
11	7
12	1
13	5
14	7
15	6

We see that

- Every die starts with a 16.6% chance of being selected
- After the first roll, the 4 sided die drops to a zero percent chance. This is because the first roll was a 6, and the four-sided die can't roll a 6
- For the first several rolls, the 6 sided die appears to have the highest likelihood, since it is the lowest numbered die that hadn't had a roll exceeding its value. But since there was an 8 rolled on roll #5, the 6 sided die dropped to zero and the 8 sided die became dominant
- The 10 and 12 sided dice experienced decaying likelihood since there was no roll greater than 8. They saw a brief spike in probability when the 6 sided die dropped out since the results would be normalized on a much smaller total probability
- The 20 sided die was the fastest to have its probability decline (except for the 4) since if we had selected a 20 sided die we were very likely to roll a large number soon and knock out most of the small numbered dice. Since that did not occur, the probability we had selected the 20 sided die was very small (but still greater than

zero)

Some things to take note of after this example

- Bayes theorem with multiple data points is basically just repeated multiplication. As a result, the final answer isn't affected by what order the data came in. If we were to roll a 1, then a 5, and then a 10 and calculate our final percentages, we would get the same final answer as if we rolled a 10, then a 5, and then a 1
- In this problem, we normalized the probabilities after every roll. You don't have to normalize each time; you could multiply all the probabilities together for each roll and normalize one time at the very end. The problem with this is that the probability numbers get very small. So small that many computer programs have trouble with numbers of that size. Truncation errors and round off errors can start to impact the results. Therefore, it tends to just be easier to normalize after each new observation than to worry about dealing with probabilities that are $1.3 * 10^{-31}$ or $2.2 * 10^{-56}$

Example 4 – Are You A Winning Player

Let's look at an example where there is a range of possible outcomes. In this example, we will try to determine how frequently a person will win at their sport. Tennis in this case. Let's say that I give you the win/loss results from 100 matches that I had. Can you tell me the probability of my long-term win rate?

For instance, if I give you results of 70 wins out of 100 matches, you could tell me that my win rate is just 70%. That is correct, but it ignores the chance that my real long-term win rate is 55%, and I just happened to get lucky and win 70 games out of 100. But in the future, I have some odds of only winning 55% of the games if I were to play another 1000.

Simply dividing will give you a single number for a result. I want to see a probability curve, i.e. something like the image below

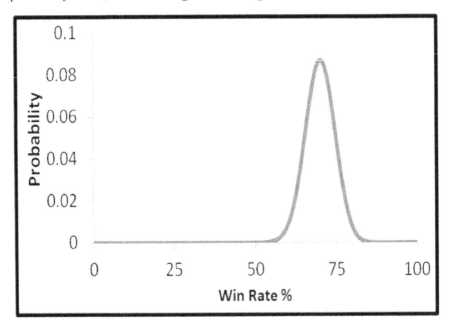

So, the question is: given that you have won 70 matches out of the last 100 matches, break the probability range into 10% segments and calculate the odds that your long-term win rate actually fall in each of those segments. To put it a different way, what are the odds that your long-term win rate is each of these percentages 0%, 10%, 20%, 30%, 40%, 50%, 60%, 70%, 80%, 90%, and 100%?

This is Sort Of Like The Binomial Theorem

The binomial theorem could give us the probability of getting different numbers of wins if we know our long-term win rate. This problem the inverse of the binomial theorem, we are looking for the probability of having different long-term win rates given that we know the number of wins. In fact, the result shown in this plot is the binomial distribution with a 70% success rate over 100 trials.

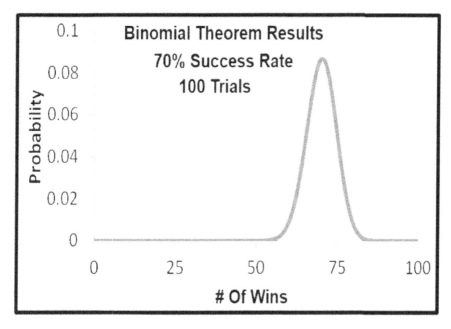

If you want to know more about the binomial distribution, look at this book "Probability With The Binomial Theorem And Pascal's Triangle"

However, this is not a binomial distribution problem. The binomial distribution would give us probabilities of the number of wins if we knew our long-term win rate. We want to know our long-term win rate given the number of wins we have. That makes it a Bayes Theorem Problem.

The Data

We don't need to generate any random data for this problem. The question tells us what we need to know, namely that there are 100 new observations, 70 of which are wins, 30 are losses. Since Bayes Theorem is just multiplication/division, and both of those operations are commutative, it doesn't matter what order those games were played in. We could have had 70 wins, then 30 losses. 30 losses, then 70 wins, or more likely that they were all interspersed.

If we wanted to solve this problem sequentially, one observation at a time, we could just generate any set of data that had 70 wins, 30 losses. However we don't actually need to solve this as 100 sequential problems (like we did with the dice example). We can incorporate all the new observations in one large step. We didn't do that for the previous problems, and won't for the following problems, to better illustrate how those examples worked. But for this example, it is easy to show it in one single step of rolling in the new information.

If you want to follow this example in the Excel that we will be showing, you can grab the EXCEL file from my website

Initial Probability

Like we see in every Bayes Theorem problem, the first step is to set up what our possible outcomes are. Then add initial probabilities. The possible outcomes are defined and are percentages from 0% to 100% by 10% steps. So there are 11 initial possibilities.

We could break the possibilities down into finer segments. Instead of 10% increments, we could do 5% increments or even 1%. However in this case that would add a lot of computation without really adding much more insight, so we will use the 10% increments.

We will naively assume that all initial possibilities have an equal probability, which is a 1 in 11 chance. This is a uniform probability distribution, and there are many other probability distributions that we could have chosen here. We could have picked a normal distribution centered around a 50% win rate, or one centered around a 70% win rate. We could have picked a triangularly shaped distribution of probabilities. What we are trying to do is pick a reasonable value. Since we don't have any solid reason for picking a different value, and to keep the example simple, we will use the uniform probability distribution.

One of the important insights to understand about Bayes Theorem is when the initial probability distribution makes a large difference. Typically estimating the prior is where there is the most opportunity for reasonable disagreement. The initial probability estimate has the largest impact when there are few data points. In this case, there are 100 new observations. So the initial probability estimate is just 1 of 101 factors that will go into the final probability. So unless we are wildly off on our initial probabilities, they will not be the determining factor in the results. This is known as "Swamping The Prior". (One common way to be wildly off on the initial probability estimate is to put a zero probability for some of the possibilities, or to not include them at all)

So this is the initial probability distribution we will use for this problem.

Long Term Win Rate Possibilities	0	0.1	0.2	0.3	0.4	0.5	0.6	0.7	0.8	0.9	1
Initial Probability	0.0909	0.0909	0.0909	0.0909	0.0909	0.0909	0.0909	0.0909	0.0909	0.0909	0.0909

Likelihood Function

Let's think about how to do the likelihood function for a single game and a single initial possibility, and then expand that to work for all 100 games and all 11 initial possibilities.

Let's say that the initial possibility that we are interested in at the moment is the 40% long-term win rate. With that, the odds of getting a win as the outcome is 0.4 multiplied by the starting probability. The odds of getting a loss as the outcome is 0.6 multiplied by the starting probability.

To generalize this process to the other possible win rates, if we were doing this calculation game by game, i.e. in 100 individual steps, we could multiply each individual cell by its respective win rate, if the outcome of that step was a win, or by (1 – win rate) if the outcome in question was a loss.

If we want to include multiple outcomes in a single step, all we need to do is include them in the multiplication. For instance, for the 40% win rate, if we wanted to include 4 wins and 1 loss, we would take the starting probability and multiply by 0.4 * 0.4 * 0.4 * 0.4 * (1-0.4). For the 80% win rate, that would be the starting probability multiplied by 0.8 * 0.8 * 0.8 * 0.8 * (1-0.8).

As a more formal equation, that looks like this

$$Initial\ Probability * Win\ Rate^{\#\ Wins} * (1 - Win\ Rate)^{\#\ Losses}$$

Since we have 70 wins and 30 losses for this example the final likelihood for the 40% win rate would be

$$Initial\ Probability * 0.4^{70} * 0.6^{30}$$

One thing we have to be careful of is to not get numeric underflow. Theoretically, the 0.4 raised to the 70th power could be a small enough number that the computer would start making errors. In this case, with the Excel version I am using, that is not an issue until we get to $1 * 10^{-307}$ which would need on the order of 300-350 games to reach.

One way to avoid this issue would be to normalize after each of the games, or after a block of games. This would ensure that the numbers would not get too small. We could also potentially avoid some of the problems by using logarithms instead of exponents, which we will see in the next example on spam filters.

Having that equation, we can solve for the probability for each of the possible initial outcomes and get this result

Long Term Win Rate Possibilities	0	0.1	0.2	0.3	0.4	0.5	0.6	0.7	0.8	0.9	1
Initial Probability	0.0909	0.0909	0.0909	0.0909	0.0909	0.0909	0.0909	0.0909	0.0909	0.0909	0.0909
After 100 Games	0.00E+00	3.85E-73	1.33E-53	5.13E-43	2.80E-36	7.17E-32	3.10E-29	2.69E-28	1.61E-29	5.70E-35	0.00E+00

70 wins, 30 losses

Unsurprisingly, since we are dealing with decimals raised to the 100th power, or so, we get really small numbers. What that is telling us is that odds of any one of these long-term win rates giving you the 70 wins and 30 losses in the order that they actually occurred is really small. This is to be expected, however, and is the same as saying that even though I know a coin will come up heads 50% of the time, I can't predict what will actually occur on the next 20 tosses.

What we really care about is how likely certain outcomes were relative to all of the other possible outcomes. To see that, we need to normalize these results.

Normalizing

Once again we normalize by finding the sum of all of the probabilities and dividing each of the probabilities by that sum. The result is

Long Term Win Rate Possibilities	0	0.1	0.2	0.3	0.4	0.5	0.6	0.7	0.8	0.9	1
Initial Probability	0.0909	0.0909	0.0909	0.0909	0.0909	0.0909	0.0909	0.0909	0.0909	0.0909	0.0909
After 100 Games	0.00E+00	3.85E-73	1.33E-54	5.13E-43	2.80E-36	7.17E-32	3.10E-29	2.69E-28	1.61E-29	5.70E-35	0.00E+00
Sum						$3.16E-28$					
Normalized Results	0.000	0.000	0.000	0.000	0.000	0.000	0.098	0.851	0.051	0.000	0.000

70 wins 30 losses

Which shows that there is an 85.1% chance that your real long-term win rate falls in the band centered around 70%, a 9.8% chance that your real long-term win rate falls in the band centered around 60%, and a 5.1% chance that your real long-term win rate falls in the band centered around 80%. The other probabilities are too small to include.

We phrased the result as "band centered around 70%" because this is a continuous range, as opposed to a discrete range. Your win rate could be 69% or 71%, it does not have to be 70% just because we picked that as our range. A good way to think about it is that each discrete win rate that we analyzed extends until the halfway point by the next win rate. I.e. the 60% range actually goes from 55%-65%. The 70% range goes from 65%-75%. So we are saying that you have an 85.1% chance that your long-term win rate is between the range of 65-75%.

Visually, we can view this result as a bar chart

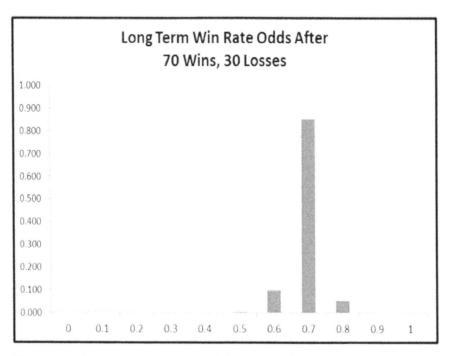

Long Term Win Rate Odds After 70 Wins, 30 Losses

Unsurprisingly, since we won 70% of the games, the most likely long-term win rate is 70%. But there is still a reasonable chance that our real long-term win rate will be more in the 60-80% range, and that some of the wins/losses were just good or bad luck.

However, it wasn't just the fact that we won 70% of our games that gave us this result. It was the fact that we did it over 100 games, which turned out to be a relatively large sample size for this analysis. If instead of having 70 wins and 30 losses, we had 7 wins and 3 losses (i.e. still 70%, but a lot smaller sample size) we would have this result

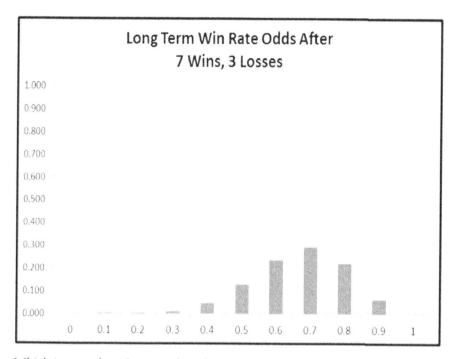

Which is a much wider spread, with much more evenly distributed probabilities.

If we played another 100 games, and also got 70 wins, 30 losses in those, then the 70% odds would become almost entirely dominant.

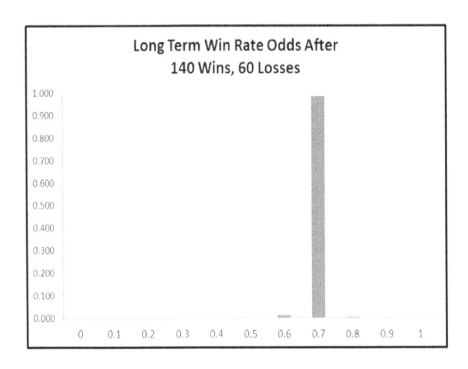

**Long Term Win Rate Odds After
140 Wins, 60 Losses**

Revisiting The Prior

At the beginning of this example, we talked about swamping the prior. I.e. getting so much data in the new observations that it doesn't really matter what probabilities you select to start with. That turns out to be the case in this example. For instance, let's say that we selected a triangular probability distribution to start with instead of a uniform distribution like we used in the results above. That would weight our win rate towards 50%, and look like the chart below

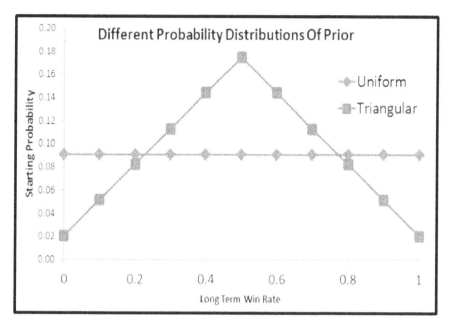

The result after 70 wins and 30 losses are final probabilities that are nearly identical, as we see in the chart below

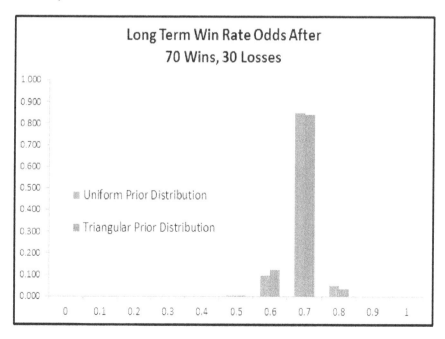

Some things to take note of after this example

The greater the difference in likelihood functions between different possibilities, the more quickly they can diverge. In this example, we saw that the differences between having a 60% win rate and a 70% win rate weren't all that high. That is why it took nearly 100 games to get a dominant possible win rate.

This is different than what we saw in the dice example. In the dice example, for instance, there was a small difference between an 8 sided and a 10 sided die when the roll was lower than an 8. However, there was a stark difference in probability when the outcome was greater than an 8. This meant that the dice could have a much more sudden divergence in probabilities than we saw in this tennis example.

Example 5 – Spam Filtering With Naïve Bayes

One area that you might have encountered Bayes Theorem without knowing it is when you are using email. Bayes was at the heart of one of the earlier (late 1990's) successful spam filters (spam is a common term for junk email). And the fact that you can use email at all is thanks to spam filters. Reasonable estimates put the number of spam emails out there as 80% or more of the total email traffic

So how is Bayes Theorem used to do spam filtering?

The high-level process is

- Figure out the spamminess of every word in an email
- Multiply all those probabilities together to determine how likely a specific email is to be spam or not spam

This process is called Naïve Bayes because it assumes independence between every word in the message. I.e. that each word contributes to the spamminess of the message independently from every other word. In reality, this isn't true since it might take an entire phrase to be spam. However, in practice, this is a useful simplification.

Let's look at the first step, calculating the spamminess of every single word. To set this up you need a data set. If you're an email provider you can generate this by seeing which emails people click "Mark as spam" on and which are treated as normal.

The spamminess of a given word can be calculated as

$$P(S|W) = \frac{P(W|S) * P(S)}{P(W|S) * P(S) + P(W|NS) * P(NS)}$$

Where

- $P(S|W)$ is the probability that a message is spam, knowing that the word "W" is in it
- $P(S)$ is the overall probability that any given message is spam

- P(W|S) is the probability that the word "W" appears in spam messages
- P(NS) is the overall probability that any given message is not spam
- P(W|NS) is the probability that the word "W" appears in non-spam messages

Which we will end up simplifying to

$$P(S|W) = \frac{P(W|S)}{P(W|S) + P(W|NS)}$$

By making a few bold assumptions.

P(s|w) is the probability that the whole message is spam given that a specific word is in the message. (s|w is short for "spam given word") This is what we will refer to as the "spamminess of that word"

What this looks like graphically is this

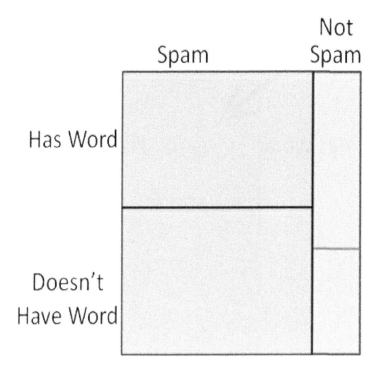

P(w|s) * P(s) is this square shown below. This is the total probability that a message has this word (P(w|s)) and that the message is spam (P(s))

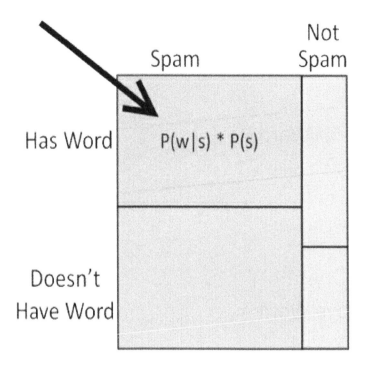

P(w|ns) * P(ns) is this square shown below. This is the total probability that a message has this word   (P(w|ns)) and that the message is not spam (P(ns))

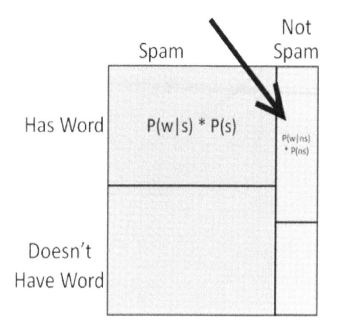

So to find the spamminess of a given word, we only care about the messages that have that word in it. We are effectively keeping the top row

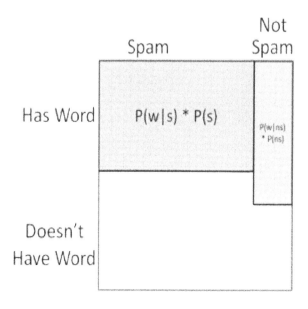

Discarding the bottom, and then asking what percentage is this square shown

below

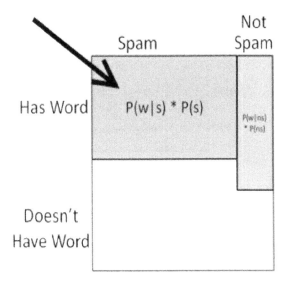

Compared to the total remaining area.

One simplification that is often made is to ignore the prior. I.e. forget that 80% of messages are spam and just assume 50% initial probability. This is basically assuming these two columns both have the same initial size.

When we make that assumption, we can take this initial equation

$$P(S|W) = \frac{P(W|S) * P(S)}{P(W|S) * P(S) + P(W|NS) * P(NS)}$$

and simplify it. First we assume that the initial probability of the word being spam or not spam are both 50%.

$$P(S|W) = \frac{P(W|S) * 0.5}{P(W|S) * 0.5 + P(W|NS) * 0.5}$$

That makes the initial probability drop out of the equation.

$$P(S|W) = \frac{P(W|S)}{P(W|S) + P(W|NS)} * 0.5$$

And since we are normalizing, we can discard the 0.5. What we are left with is

$$P(S|W) = \frac{P(W|S)}{P(W|S) + P(W|NS)}$$

As words, the right side of the equation gives the spamminess of a word by

$$= \frac{\% \text{ Of Time In Spam}}{(\% \text{ Of Time In Spam}) + (\% \text{ Of Time Not In Spam})}$$

Which is the same as

$$= \frac{\# \text{ Of Times In Spam}}{(\# \text{ Of Times In Spam}) + (\# \text{ Of Times Not In Spam})}$$

So the spamminess of a word can be calculated by just

- Counting how many time a word appears in spam messages
- Counting how many times the word appears in total
- Taking the ratio of the total spam count to the sum of both counts

The ideal result from this is that words which are neutral (i.e. neither indicate not contraindicate spam, such as "the", "and", "at") end up near 50%. Words that are unlikely to indicate spam end up near 0%, and words that are very likely to indicate spam (i.e. Viagra) end up near 100%.

To do this, the Naïve Bayes classifier should be trained on a set that is 50% composed of spam and 50%, not spam. Or adjustments should be made to the results so that neutral words lie at a 50% spamminess level.

How To Get The Spamminess Of The Whole Message

Once the spamminess of individual words is established, the next step is to calculate the spamminess of a message overall, given the words it contains. The formula for this is

$$p = \frac{p_1 * p_2 * \dots * p_N}{(p_1 * p_2 * \dots * p_N) + (1 - p_1)(1 - p_2) \dots (1 - p_N)}$$

Where p is the probability that a message is spam. And p# is the percentage of time that a given word appears in spam messages.

Let's see how this formula works for a single world. This word has a spamminess of 0.9. So the total message has a spamminess of

$$p = \frac{0.9}{0.9 + (1 - 0.9)} = \frac{0.9}{0.9 + 0.1} = \frac{0.9}{1.0} = 0.9$$

Unsurprisingly, the message has a spamminess of 0.9

With two words, let's say 0.9 and 0.6, the equation is

$$p = \frac{0.9 * 0.6}{0.9 * 0.6 + (1 - 0.9)(1 - 0.6)}$$

$$p = \frac{0.54}{0.54 + 0.04} = \frac{0.54}{0.58} = 0.931$$

So adding a secondly slightly spammy word increased the spamminess of the message. What we see with the ratio is that .54 is the probability that a message containing both words is spam. The .04 is the probability that a message containing both words is not spam.

So why don't those numbers sum to 1.0? After all, with 1 word the 0.9 and the 0.1 summed to 1.0. However, since we are multiplying the probabilities we are getting very smaller odds. Effectively what we see is that many messages which contain the first word don't contain the second word. In this case, since we multiplied the original spam area from the first word (of 0.9) by .6 and the original non-spam area from the first word (of 0.1) by 0.4, the non-spam area shrunk by more. I.e. including the second word made it more likely that the message is spam.

As we keep adding words, both the spam and non-spam values become vanishingly small. However what matters is the relative probability between spam and non-spam. I.e. which value is getting smaller faster?

What Do We Do With The Final Probability?

The final result from our equation is a probability that the message is spam. If that probability is above a certain threshold, say 0.95, the message is marked as spam by the software and likely moved to a special spam folder. Otherwise, it is assumed to be a legitimate message.

Numeric Underflow

One issue with this equation is numeric underflow. If you multiply a bunch of probabilities together, eventually you get a number so small that the computer will round to zero, or make other errors.

Since a message can have an infinite number of words, and each of those words has a probability, this is an issue. Fortunately the equation

$$p = \frac{p_1 * p_2 * \ldots * p_N}{(p_1 * p_2 * \ldots * p_N) + (1 - p_1)(1 - p_2) \ldots (1 - p_N)}$$

Can be rearranged to not use the product of a string of numbers. What allows us to do this is logarithms. Since

$$log(A * B * C) = log(A) + log(B) + log(C)$$

This works no matter what the base of the logarithm is, whether it is base 10, base 2, the natural log, etc. Without going into too much detail, we can take the original equation and invert it

$$\frac{1}{p} = \frac{(p_1 * p_2 * ... * p_N) + (1 - p_1)(1 - p_2)...(1 - p_N)}{(p_1 * p_2 * ... * p_N)}$$

Then simplify the fraction on the right side

$$\frac{1}{p} = 1 + \frac{(1 - p_1)(1 - p_2)...(1 - p_N)}{(p_1 * p_2 * ... * p_N)}$$

Rearrange the equation by pulling one of the terms onto the left side

$$\frac{1}{p} - 1 = \frac{(1 - p_1)(1 - p_2)...(1 - p_N)}{(p_1 * p_2 * ... * p_N)}$$

Take the natural logarithm of both sides

$$\ln\left(\frac{1}{p} - 1\right) = \ln(1 - p_1) + \ln(1 - p_2) + \cdots + \ln(1 - p_N) \\ - \ln(p_1) - \ln(p_2) - \cdots - \ln(p_N)$$

Just to simplify the equation, we can set M equal to the right side of the equation

$$M = \ln(1 - p_1) + \ln(1 - p_2) + \cdots + \ln(1 - p_N) \\ - \ln(p_1) - \ln(p_2) - \cdots - \ln(p_N)$$

And we get

$$\ln\left(\frac{1}{p} - 1\right) = M$$

Then take the inverse of the natural logarithm (e) of both sides, without simplifying the right side of the equation. (This is important since we want to keep the equation as a sum instead of a product).

$$\frac{1}{p} - 1 = e^M$$

Then rearrange to pull the term back on the right side

$$\frac{1}{p} = e^M + 1$$

And invert the results

$$p = \frac{1}{e^M + 1}$$

This is the final result, recalling the M is the sum and difference of the logarithms that we defined earlier.

$$M = \ln(1 - p_1) + \ln(1 - p_2) + \cdots + \ln(1 - p_N)$$
$$- \ln(p_1) - \ln(p_2) - \cdots - \ln(p_N)$$

We really didn't do anything to the equation. We just did a few simplifications and rearranging steps, and then undid everything except without simplifying our logarithm and inverse logarithm. So this is the exact same equation that we originally had for finding the spamminess of the full message, except it doesn't have the risk of numeric underflow.

Refinements to Naïve Bayes

One refinement to this Naïve Bayes equation for spam checking is to only look at the words that are the most or least spammy. I.e. instead of evaluating the equation to determine the spamminess of the entire message using every single word, use the 20 words that have the biggest impact on the analysis, or the top 10% most impactful words, or a similar metric.

The equation to determine which words have the largest impact is

$$\left| P_i - 0.5 \right|$$

Where Pi is the spamminess score of any given word.

This can improve the results by ignoring the vast majority of the words that will have little impact, and instead focusing on the most important words.

More Refinement To This Technique

Instead of a single word, this technique can be applied to multiple words. I.e. treat a 3-word string as a single object. So instead of using "Buy Viagra Now" as three separate words, it can be analyzed with a single spamminess score. This can increase the accuracy of the results, but also greatly increases the size of the database required to store the spamminess scores.

Ways To Work Around The Naïve Bayes Spam Filter

Unsurprisingly people are always trying to bypass spam filters, and some techniques have been developed which work to varying degrees. The most basic technique is probably to use misspellings of the spam words. You've probably seen that. I.e. instead of "Buy Viagra" you would see a message of "Buy V1agra"

You still know what it means, but the "1" instead of the "i" makes it a new word. This is a poor attempt though because fairly soon the spam filter will learn that each specific misspelling is a spam word. And there are only so many variations you can do before a word is unreadable.

Bayesian Poisoning

A more sophisticated countermeasure is called Baycsian Poisoning. This attempts to reduce the spamminess of the overall message by including a bunch of non-spammy words. I.e. I might be able to get away with including a very spammy word, such as "Viagra" (with a hypothetical score of 0.95) if I can find a couple of words with low spamminess scores to balance it out. Maybe "Canada" or a different friendly word.

The trick, of course, is knowing what those non-spammy words are. I could load up the message with a bunch of words and hope it gets through. For instance, maybe put "Buy Viagra Here" at the top of the message and then copy a news article below it.

That technique tends to be marginally effective. However, it can be very effective if the spammer can get feedback about which emails get through. (Making it active spamming where the spam messages are refined, rather than passive where they are just sent out)

In that case, the technique is to send out many emails with the spam and some text to make the message less spammy, find out which messages go through, and then flood the system with variations of those messages.

That technique requires the spammers to know which emails get delivered. That is why most email systems default to not showing web images in an email. (i.e. you might have to click to enable images) Nor do anything else that would give feedback. If those images were automatically loaded, then anytime you opened a spam email, the spammer would know that they reached you, and could use that knowledge to send you and others more spam.

Example 6 – More Dice, But With Errors In The Data Stream
Up until now, we've assumed that every new observation is valid. That allowed us to do things such as set the probability of a die equal to zero if any roll exceeded the number of sides that die has. But not all input is good. A person can write down the wrong die roll. A person can mark an email as spam when it isn't. Bayes Theorem can account for these possibilities by modifying our likelihood function, which we will see in this example.

The setup for this example is the same as problem 2, except that we are going to assume there could be errors in our data. Our friend is pulling a die out of a bag again, and the die could have 4, 6, 8, 10, 12, or 20 sides. He is going to roll the die 80 times and write down the results.

The only problem is that this time he is sloppy at writing down the results. Perhaps he is a bad typist and his fingers keep slipping on the keyboard. As a result, 95% of the time the data will be entered correctly, but the other 5% of the time the data we are working with will just be a random number between 1 and 20.

Data Generation

As input, I entered the number of sides on the selected die, as well as the odds that the data had an error. In this case, the die rolled is an 8 sided die, and there is a 5% chance of an error.

To generate the input in Excel, I used a combination of these functions

- IF()
- RAND()
- RANDBETWEEN()

The pseudocode I used to generate the rolls is

= IF(RAND() > Probability of Error, RANDBETWEEN(1, # of Sides on Die), RANDBETWEEN(1,20))

Which says:

- First, generate a random number between 0 and 1 (using Rand())
- if the random number is greater than the probability of an error (.05 in this example) then there was not an error on this roll, so

> generate a random integer between 1 and the number of sides on the die
- Otherwise, generate a random integer between 1 and 20

The EXCEL file with the data and solution is available here, the 80 die rolls that I used are

5, 6, 1, 7, 2, 2, 6, 3, 3, 6

4, 5, 1, 7, 7, 6, 7, 3, 4, 1

7, 4, 3, 3, 2, 7, 2, 7, 3, 6

8, 4, 1, 2, 6, 6, 1, 4, 3, 1

2, 4, 7, 6, 3, 8, 4, 5, 8, 7

4, 8, 3, 7, 4, 1, 6, 5, 8, 7

3, 7, 17, 5, 6, 1, 4, 8, 7, 3

2, 3, 5, 7, 6, 3, 4, 19, 1, 4

(Side-note, what do you think your error rate for manually copying those numbers down for your own use is? 1-2% ?)

What If You Ignored The Possibility of An Error?

At first thought, we could solve this problem just like we did in the previous example. That method is: if a roll is greater than the number of sides on the die, set the Likelihood of that die to zero. Otherwise set the likelihood of that die to 1 divided by the number of sides on the die. But when you do that, the plot of probabilities becomes what is shown below.

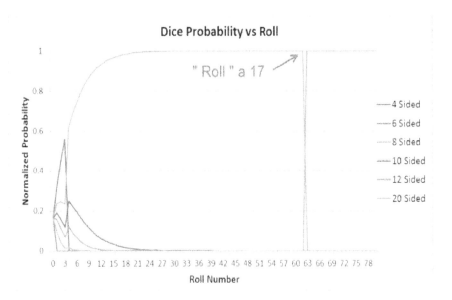

Dice Probability vs Roll

"Roll" a 17

Legend:
4 Sided
6 Sided
8 Sided
10 Sided
12 Sided
20 Sided

Y-axis: Normalized Probability
X-axis: Roll Number

What occurs here is that the 8 sided die becomes dominant within the first 20 rolls, which are all less than 8.   By roll number 63 the 8 sided die is extremely dominant, and the odds of the next closest die, which is the 10, are less than 1 in 1 million.

However the odds of getting an error are only 1 in 20, and when an error occurs, the odds that the number written down will be will be greater than 8 is 60% (12 in 20). So 3% of the rolls will be an error greater than 8, which is what happens on roll #63 where a 17 is "rolled".

Since the likelihood equation is set up to set the odds of a die equal to zero whenever a number greater than it is rolled, the odds for everything except the 20 sided die go to zero, which makes the normalized odds for the 20 sided die 100%

Now if a person was scrupulously watching the data, they might spot the error and cut the 17 from the dataset. But they might not. A more robust way is to bake some possible error into the conditional probability equations. The high level thought process behind this is

Never set any probability to zero unless you are positive that it cannot occur and you want to cut it from any future consideration.

This is important and bears repeating. If you set any probability equal to zero (either likelihood or prior) it is gone forever. If instead you just set it equal to a small number, it can still come back given enough data. We see this in medical tests, where we account for a false positive and false negative rate. (A humorous example of setting the prior equal to zero can be found on this SMBC comic – Bayesian Vampire)

If you do set the conditional probabilities to zero, then you could have a scenario where you roll one thousand numbers between 1 and 8, but the one thousand and the first number gets written down as a 9 and you would strike the 8 from the possibilities. If instead of setting the conditional probabilities to zero, you just set it to a really small number, then the initial 1000 rolls would overwhelm the 1001st roll which is an error.

So how should the equations be set up?

Initial Probabilities

Once again we are setting the initial probabilities for each die to be 1 in 6

Dice Possibilities	4	6	8	10	12	20
Initial Probability	0.166667	0.166667	0.166667	0.166667	0.166667	0.166667

Likelihood Function

The conditional probabilities are what is different from the previous die example. But we are still setting up the equation as "IF the roll is greater than the number on the die, use one probability, otherwise use a different probability". So all we need to do is calculate what the two likelihood probabilities are, baking our error rate into the equation. The two probabilities that we need to calculate are

- If the recorded number is greater than the number on the die, what are the odds you would have gotten that recorded number if you had selected that die from the bag
- If the recorded number is less than the number on the die, what are the odds you would have gotten that recorded number if you had selected that die from the bag

I am going to explain the equations using a 6 sided die as an example. And the same equations would be applied separately for the other dice.

Scenario 1: If the recorded number is greater than 6, for instance, if it is a 7

If you had a 6 sided die, the odds of recording a 7 are the probability of recording an error, divided by 20. This is because the only way you can get a number greater than the die is if it is an error, so we start with the error rate. And if the recorded number is an error, the odds that it will be any given number are 1 in 20. That probability gets multiplied by the probability of the previous die roll or initial probability.

Scenario 2: If the recorded number is less than 6, for instance, if it is a 2

If you had a 6 sided die, the odds of recording a 2 are one minus the probability of an error (i.e. the probability of correctly recording the die roll) divided by the number of sides on the die (6 in this case) PLUS the probability of recording an error divided by 20.

These odds are because there are two ways of recording a 2 for this 6 sided die. The first is that you roll a 2, and correctly record it. In that case, the probability a 2 is written down is 1/6 * the probability of correctly recording the die roll. The second way of recording a 2 is to roll any number, and then incorrectly record it and randomly write down a 2.

This could be confusing, but you could actually use the 6 sided die, roll a 2, and then ignore the roll but still randomly write down a 2. I.e. one way to think about it is that when you make an error, 5% of the time in this problem, you don't even bother looking at the die roll and just write down a random number.

That total probability gets multiplied by the probability of the previous die roll or initial probability.

A different way of arriving at the conditional probability equation

If the conditional probability equation with the error doesn't make sense, here is a different way of thinking about it.

- Start with the conditional probability for when there is no error. i.e. a 0% chance if the roll is greater than the number on the die,

and 1 divided by the number on the die otherwise
- Then subtract the probability of writing down an error from the 1 divided by the die number. I.e. if you write down an error 5% of the time, the probability of not writing down the error is .95, which is then multiplied by the 1 divided by the die number
- Then, for both parts of the if statement, add in the probability that you would write down an error divided by 20 (since if you write down an error, there is a 1 in 20 chance you would write down any given number)

The Results

When you incorporate the likelihood function which accounts for an error into all of the dice, and all of the rolls, and normalize, as usual, the results are

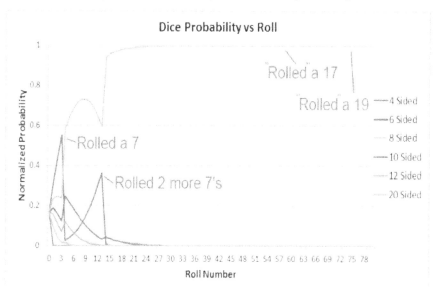

In this example, the 6 sided die initially is the favorite, because the first 3 rolls are 5, 6, 1. Then a 7 is rolled and the 8 sided die is the favorite. However, in this example, the 7 doesn't make the probability of having a 6 sided die completely equal to 0 because that 7 could be an error.

For the next nine rolls, they are all less than or equal to 6, and the 6 sided die starts to rise in probability again. However, then there are two 7's rolled in quick succession and the probability of having the 6 sided die becomes very small.

Later on, there is a 17 and a 19 rolled that are clearly an error. Without the error checking the 20 sided die would become the only possibility. But with the error checking the 8 sided die is still the most likely.

For the previous example, we used a fairly low error rate, only 5%. At that level of error, a person could likely manually review data and spot unusual numbers, which is basically what we were doing with this chart when we determined that it was weird for the 8 sided die to take such a hit

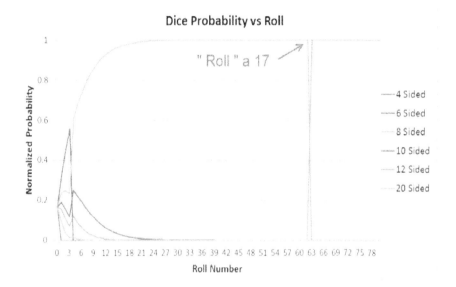

But what if you had a much higher error rate? This example is the same as the previous example, except instead of a 5% error rate, we are assuming a 75% error rate. Since we have such a high error rate, we also need more data, so we have 250 rolls of the dice instead of 80. Once again we are starting with an 8 sided die as the die actually drawn from the bag

The data that I am using is (listed left to right, and then down to the next row)

9, 8, 16, 3, 8, 4, 3, 6, 3, 18, 9, 17, 18, 5, 13, 8, 7, 6, 4, 2
11, 17, 17, 5, 14, 12, 6, 12, 6, 6, 3, 6, 6, 13, 13, 5, 4, 2, 6, 4
2, 3, 1, 8, 16, 4, 1, 11, 8, 7, 14, 16, 5, 10, 2, 3, 8, 2, 1, 3
10, 6, 16, 6, 10, 17, 1, 18, 19, 4, 5, 7, 3, 4, 2, 4, 20, 14, 20, 10
16, 6, 1, 7, 5, 1, 15, 8, 7, 1, 12, 10, 13, 1, 6, 9, 11, 13, 7, 15
10, 14, 6, 3, 5, 6, 1, 6, 2, 13, 20, 5, 18, 1, 12, 10, 10, 4, 5, 16
5, 14, 3, 4, 4, 2, 11, 12, 18, 4, 8, 1, 5, 19, 14, 7, 14, 17, 16, 8
1, 20, 18, 4, 5, 1, 7, 4, 5, 13, 8, 17, 3, 7, 6, 16, 18, 2, 11, 6

10, 19, 13, 2, 7, 12, 11, 18, 12, 4, 10, 8, 3, 10, 14, 18, 16, 3, 15, 11
16, 14, 7, 7, 13, 12, 11, 2, 6, 19, 7, 3, 19, 1, 5, 19, 18, 3, 18, 7
4, 4, 11, 14, 12, 5, 1, 12, 8, 19, 5, 19, 14, 16, 18, 9, 7, 3, 18, 2
5, 8, 1, 15, 11, 14, 19, 6, 4, 19, 3, 15, 11, 6, 18, 17, 13, 17, 9, 7
7, 15, 3, 15, 16, 16, 20, 2, 2, 5

Here it is not so easy to tell which items in the data are in error

Applying the same likelihood equation, which accounts for possible errors to this dataset, the plot below gets generated

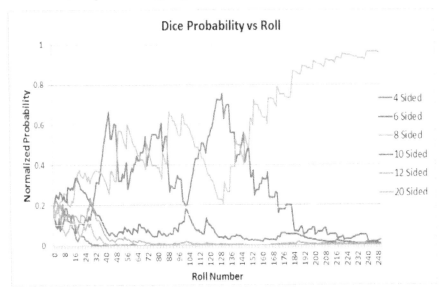

Once again the 8 sided die becomes the most likely die that was drawn from the bag. With this high error rate, it took many more rolls, and the result was a lot choppier. However, even after an only moderate number of rolls, the result was most likely either the 6 or the 8, with the 10 being a smaller possibility.

If you have an even higher error rate, for instance, 99%, you could still get the correct answer out of it. However, the higher the error rate, the more rolls you will need. For this 75% error rate, we are getting 1 good data point out of every 4. If we had a 99% error rate, we would get 1 good data point out of every 100, so we would likely need at least 25 times as much data as we have now to get a dominant die.

What if you don't know the probability of an error?

Part of my solution in these examples could be considered cheating. After all, I input the probability of the error, so, therefore, I knew exactly how likely there was to be an error and could bake that into the likelihood equations. What if you didn't know the likelihood of the error? After all, if you are working with actual data from actual measurements, you would have at best a rough guess as to what your error rate was.

For these plots, I'm going to use the same dice rolls as I used in the previous examples. Those charts were generated with the 5% error rate and the 75% error rate respectively. However, I am going to vary the error rate that is built into the conditional probability equations to be something different.

For the 5% error rate data, this was the baseline plot, which we generated knowing there was a 5% error rate

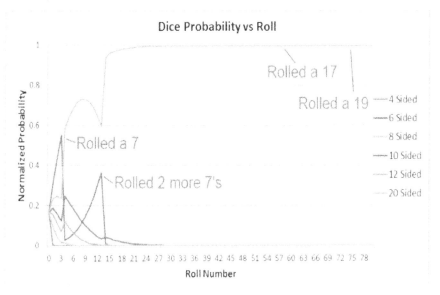

If instead we mistakenly assume there is a 1% error rate the plot changes to be

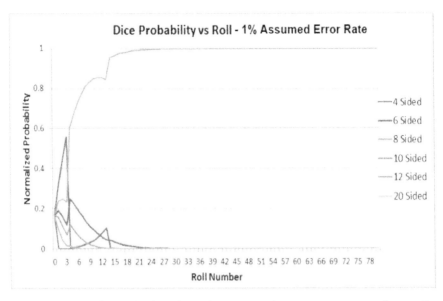

This is very similar to the baseline plot, except that it is converging faster. In fact, we can knock the guessed error rate down even further, and get substantially the same result

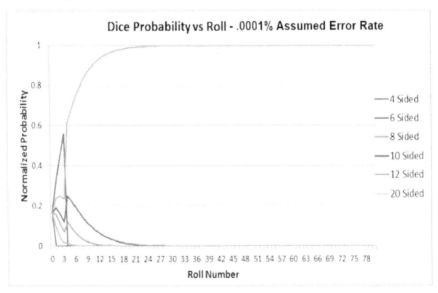

This plot is guessing a .0001% error rate. It looks almost exactly like the plot would if we assumed no errors and then actually did not have any errors. This is because by rolls 63 and 78 when we are getting our error rolls of 17

and 19, the probability of the other numbers are so low that even assuming a very low error rate doesn't change the results.

It is, however, possible to guess an error rate so low that the results change on this plot. Here is the plot using the ridiculously low error rate of 1e-25

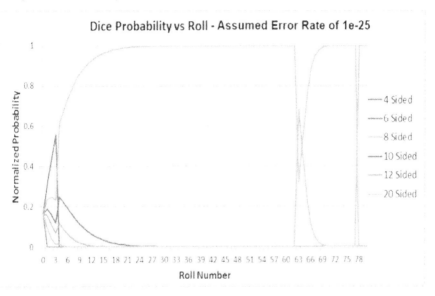

So clearly if we set the error rate too low the results change and end up being the same as if we had not included an error rate at all. In this case "too low" is "ridiculously low", but that would not be true for every problem.

What happens if we overestimate our error rate? Here the error rate is assumed to be 10% when it was generated at 5%.

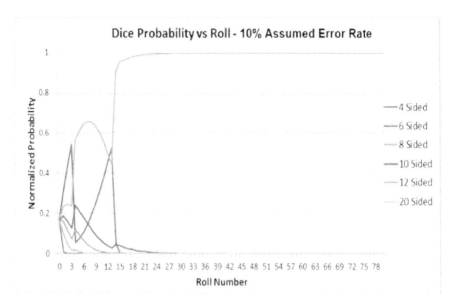

Dice Probability vs Roll - 10% Assumed Error Rate

We start to see a slower convergence towards the 8 sided die, and a greater likelihood of the 6 sided die until it got knocked out of the running by multiple 7's right in a row.

Here we are assuming the error rate is 50%.

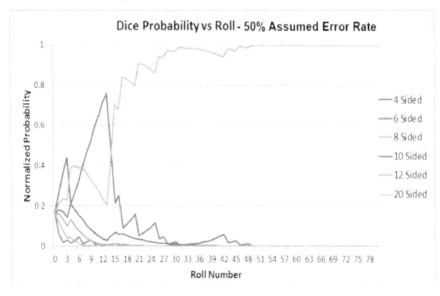

Dice Probability vs Roll - 50% Assumed Error Rate

And we start to see it take quite a bit longer to converge, although it does converge on the correct solution.

Those were examples where the actual error rate was low, 5%. What about when the actual error rate is high, 75%? This is the plot of the baseline problem, where the data was generated with a 75% error rate, and the conditional probabilities were correctly done with the 75% error rate

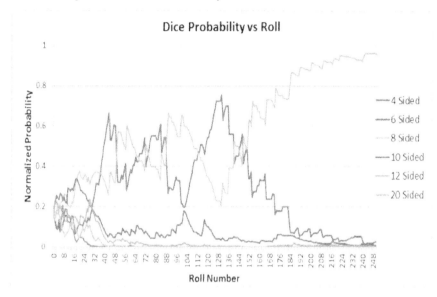

If instead, we generate the data with the 75% error rate but guess that the error rate is 5% our result is

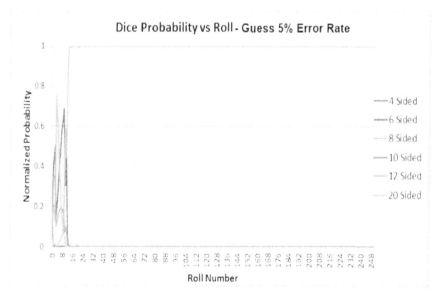

That result is wrong. It calculated the 20 sided die as the one selected, which is not correct. Even if we guess a 50% error rate on the data that was generated with the 75% error rate, it still trends to the wrong answer of the 20 sided die

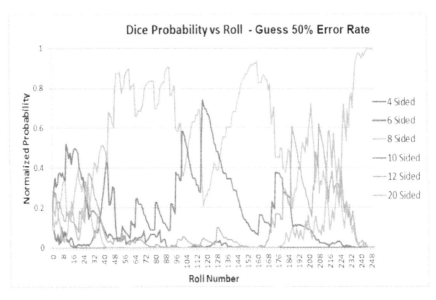

If we guess high and guess an error rate of 90% we get the following chart

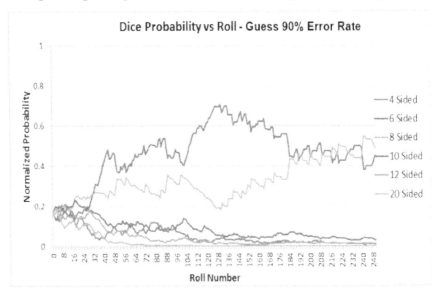

This shows the 6 and 8 sided die as having the highest probability, but it has not yet converged as having one die have the dominant results yet.

Big Picture Takeaway

So what is the big takeaway from all these charts of the sensitivity around different error rates?

- If your estimate of the error rate is higher than the actual error rate, the results will converge slower but will still converge to the correct result
- If you estimate the error rate too low there is a risk that the results will not be correct
- The smaller the actual error rate is, the more wiggle room you have in guessing the error rate
- The higher the actual error rate is, the more data you need

Example 7 – The German Tank Problem

One of the most famous historical applications of Bayes Theorem is the German Tank Problem. In this problem, you are trying to estimate how many tanks have been produced by the enemy, based off of the serial numbers of captured tanks. Bayes theorem was used in World War 2 by the Allies to do exactly that, and ended up with results that were substantially lower for a total number of tanks produced by Axis countries than conventional intelligence estimates (i.e. spies) were reporting. After the war, records indicated that the statistical estimates using Bayes Theorem were also substantially more correct.

In real life, efforts can be made to obfuscate serial numbers, and pick non-sequential numbers, or to use random starting points. However, there are also multiple components that serial numbers could be drawn from, such as gun barrels, wheels, seats, engines, etc. This makes it more of a military intelligence problem than the pure math that we will show.

Problem

You are analyzing serial numbers pulled off of wrecked or captured tanks. Use those numbers to estimate how many tanks have been produced. You know this about the tank serial numbers

- They start at 1
- They are sequential without gaps

You have found these serial numbers, 30, 70, 140, 125

Setting Up The Problem

Of all the examples in this book, this is the one where there is the most opportunity for differences in both the problem setup and the initial estimate or probabilities. The biggest question to ask is, what is the maximum number of tanks in the estimate?

For this problem, I am going to choose a maximum of 1,000 tanks. But a reasonable person could choose a different number such as 500 tanks, or 2,000 tanks and get different results. Because I am solving this problem in Excel, I am going to analyze for every 20 tanks (I.e. calculate the odds of having 20, 40, 60, 80 etc. tanks), which means I have 50 initial possibilities for numbers of tanks.   You could analyze for every single number in Excel with some difficulty, or do it easily in a programming language, but making this assumption will give more or less the same answer and substantially reduce the size of the Excel sheet.

Like we have seen in other problems, we will give each possibility its own column in Excel, and each new observed outcome its own row.

Example 7

You are analyzing serial numbers pulled off of wrecked or captured tanks.
Use those numbers to estimate how many tanks have been produced.

You know this about the tank serial numbers
They start at 1
- They are sequential without gaps
You have found these serial numbers: 30, 70, 140, 125

Tank Number	Serial Number	Total Number of Tanks	20	40	60	80	100	120
0		Initial Probability	1	1	1	1	1	1
1	30	Tank 1	0.00000	0.00050	0.00033	0.00025	0.00020	0.00017
2	70	Tank 2	0.00000	0.00000	0.00000	0.00089	0.00057	0.00040
3	140	Tank 3	0.00000	0.00000	0.00000	0.00000	0.00000	0.00000
4	125	Tank 4	0.00000	0.00000	0.00000	0.00000	0.00000	0.00000

I am assuming that all possibilities of the number of tanks have an equal initial probability (i.e. in the prior there is the same probability of having 50 tanks as having 500 tanks).   Once again, this is something that a reasonable person could make a different assumption on, and get different results. (Note, there are more columns in the Excel file than shown in the picture, it wasn't possible to show all the way up to 1000 and still make the picture legible)

Likelihood Function

The conditional probability is a lot like the conditional probability for the dice problem.

- If the serial number observed is greater than the max serial number for that possibility, the probability of having that number of tanks is 0
- If the serial number observed is less than the max serial number for that possibility, the probability of observing that number is 1

> divided by that number of tanks, multiplied by the probability for
> the previous step

To keep this problem simple, I'm ignoring any possible error in our observations.

After multiplying these conditional probabilities through the 4 tanks observed and normalizing, these are the results

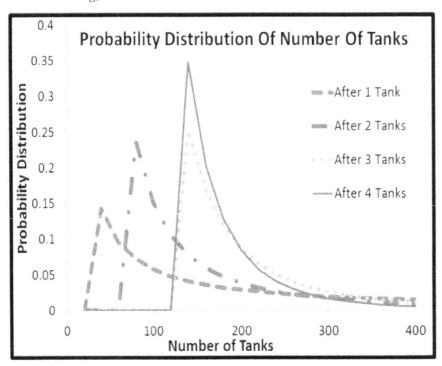

There is a big spike in probability at the maximum serial number observed. After that, there is an asymptotic decay towards the greater number of tanks. After 4 tanks, the maximum number observed is 140, so the single most likely answer is that there are 140 tanks. The location of that spike changes as the maximum observed serial number changes for different observations.

Based on this result, a person might estimate that there are 140 tanks. However, even though that number is the most likely answer, it is not the best estimate since it is almost definitely under-predicting the number of tanks.

If we take a weighted average of the number of tanks (i.e. multiply 140 tanks by its final probability, 160 tanks by its final probability, 180 by its probability, etc., and sum that result) we get a total of 193.3 tanks, which is a good estimate for the total number of tanks.

If we had assumed 2,000 tanks at the beginning, the weighted average would be 195.4 tanks, which is substantially the same result.

Made in the USA
Monee, IL
23 June 2021